TIP 1: CLAIM AND OPTIMIZE YOUR GOOGLE BUSINESS PROFILE

One of the foundational steps for any business looking to establish a strong online presence is to claim and optimize your Google Business Profile. This is a free tool provided by Google that allows you to manage how your business appears in Google Search and Google Maps.

Here's how to get started:

1. **Claim Your Profile:** If you haven't already, claim your business on Google by going to the Google Business Profile website and following the verification process. This ensures that you have control over the information displayed about your business.

2. **Complete Your Profile:** Fill out all the essential information, including your business name, address, phone number, website, and business hours. Be thorough and accurate in providing this information to help potential customers find and contact you.

3. **Add High-Quality Photos:** Upload high-resolution images of your business, including the exterior, interior, products, and services. Visual content can significantly impact a customer's decision to visit your business.

4. **Write a Compelling Business Description:** Craft a concise and engaging business description that highlights your unique selling points and what sets your business apart from the competition.

5. **Encourage Customer Reviews:** Positive reviews on your Google Business Profile can boost your credibility and attract more customers. Encourage happy customers to leave reviews, and always respond to reviews promptly and professionally.

6. **Use Posts and Updates:** Take advantage of the Posts feature to share news, events, promotions, and other updates with your audience. These posts appear prominently in your profile and can help you stay engaged with potential customers.

By claiming and optimizing your Google Business Profile, you'll improve your online visibility, provide accurate information to customers, and create a positive impression that can drive more foot traffic and online inquiries to your business. This is just the first step toward leveraging the power of Google's tools for business success.

TIP 2: CONSISTENTLY MONITOR AND UPDATE YOUR BUSINESS INFORMATION

Once you've claimed and optimized your Google Business Profile, the next crucial step is to consistently monitor and update your business information. Here's why this is essential:

1. **Accurate Information:** Your business details, such as hours of operation, phone number, and address, should always reflect the current situation. When potential customers search for your business, they rely on this information to make decisions. Outdated or incorrect data can lead to frustration and lost opportunities.

2. **Special Hours:** Keep your profile updated with special hours for holidays, events, or unexpected closures. This ensures that customers are informed and helps you maintain a positive reputation.

3. **COVID-19 Updates:** During times of crisis, like the COVID-19 pandemic, Google Business Profiles played a crucial role in communicating safety measures and changes in business operations. Regularly update your profile to provide accurate information about safety protocols, online ordering, or any other relevant updates related to the current environment.

4. **Engage with Customer Questions:** Monitor and respond to customer questions and inquiries promptly. This demonstrates your commitment to customer service and can influence potential customers positively.

5. **Utilize Insights:** Google provides valuable insights about how users interact with your profile, including how many people viewed your profile, requested directions, or visited your website. Use these insights to make data-driven decisions and refine your profile for better performance.

6. **Add New Photos and Posts:** Keep your profile fresh by adding new photos that showcase your latest products, services, or offerings. Regularly post updates, promotions, and announcements to keep your audience engaged. (At least once a week)

7. **Check for Duplicates:** Occasionally, duplicate or incorrect profiles can appear for your business. Regularly search for duplicates and report them to Google to maintain the integrity of your online presence.

By staying vigilant and proactive in monitoring and updating your Google Business Profile, you ensure that potential customers receive accurate and up-to-date information about your business. This can help you build trust, attract more customers, and maintain a competitive edge in the online marketplace. In the ever-evolving digital landscape, a well-maintained profile is a valuable asset for your business.

TIP 3: LEVERAGE GOOGLE MY BUSINESS POSTS FOR PROMOTIONS AND ENGAGEMENT

Google My Business (GMB) Posts are a powerful tool for businesses to engage with their audience and promote their products or services. Here's how you can make the most of GMB Posts:

1. **Create Compelling Posts:** Craft eye-catching and informative posts that highlight your latest promotions, products, events, or news. Use high-quality images, clear text, and a strong call to action to encourage user engagement.

2. **Choose Post Types:** Google offers several post types, such as "What's New," "Events," "Offers," and "Products." Select the most relevant type for your content to provide context to your audience.

3. **Use Keywords:** Incorporate relevant keywords in your posts to improve their visibility in Google searches. Think about the terms your potential customers might use when looking for your products or services.

4. **Include Links:** Posts allow you to include links to specific pages on your website, making it easy for customers to learn more about your offerings or make a purchase.

5. **Add Booking and Order Links:** If applicable, include direct links for customers to book appointments or place orders online. This streamlines the process and can lead to higher conversion rates.

6. **Utilize Event Posts:** If you're hosting events or webinars, create event posts to provide all the necessary details, including date, time, location (virtual or physical), and registration links.

7. **Highlight Customer Reviews:** Showcase positive customer reviews in your posts to build trust and credibility with potential customers.

8. **Regular Posting Schedule:** Consistency is key. Establish a regular posting schedule to keep your audience engaged and informed about your latest offerings and updates.

9. **Track Performance:** Use the insights provided by Google to assess the performance of your posts. This data can help you refine your posting strategy and tailor your content to what resonates most with your audience.

Google My Business Posts are a dynamic way to keep your audience informed and engaged while promoting your business. They appear prominently in your Google Business Profile, making them a valuable tool for attracting and retaining customers. By mastering the art of GMB Posts, you can maximize the impact of your online presence and stand out in search results.

TIP 4: ENCOURAGE AND RESPOND TO CUSTOMER REVIEWS EFFECTIVELY

Customer reviews can significantly influence potential customers' decisions, so it's essential to actively encourage and respond to reviews on your Google Business Profile. Here's how to do it effectively:

1. **Encourage Reviews:** Politely ask satisfied customers to leave reviews on your Google Business Profile. Make the request at the right time, such as after a successful transaction or positive interaction. Explain how their reviews can benefit your business and help others make informed choices.

2. **Monitor Reviews:** Regularly check your profile for new reviews. Google provides notifications, but it's a good practice to proactively monitor your profile to stay on top of feedback.

3. **Thank Reviewers:** Always express gratitude to customers

who leave positive reviews. A simple "thank you" shows appreciation for their support and encourages them to continue their patronage.

4. **Respond Promptly:** Address negative reviews promptly and professionally. Listen to the customer's concerns, empathize with their experience, and offer a solution or steps to resolve the issue. Maintain a positive and solution-oriented tone.

5. **Keep It Personal:** Avoid generic responses. Personalize your replies to show that you genuinely care about each customer's experience.

6. **Highlight Positive Feedback:** Use positive reviews as testimonials on your website and marketing materials. This reinforces your credibility and can influence potential customers.

7. **Address Constructive Criticism:** Even negative reviews can provide valuable insights for improvement. Use constructive criticism as an opportunity to enhance your products, services, or customer experience.

8. **Stay Professional:** Always maintain professionalism in your responses, regardless of the tone of the review. Responding with courtesy and professionalism reflects well on your business.

9. **Flag Inappropriate Content:** If you come across reviews that violate Google's review policies, such as fake reviews or

inappropriate content, flag them for removal.

10. **Engage with Positive Feedback:** Engage with positive reviews by asking follow-up questions or encouraging customers to share their experience with others. This can lead to more positive word-of-mouth marketing.

Effective management of customer reviews not only enhances your online reputation but also demonstrates your commitment to customer satisfaction. Positive reviews can attract new customers, while thoughtful responses to negative reviews can help salvage customer relationships and improve your business's overall image. By creating a feedback loop with your customers through reviews, you can continuously refine your offerings and provide an exceptional customer experience.

TIP 5: USE GOOGLE Q&A TO ADDRESS CUSTOMER QUERIES

Google Q&A is a valuable feature of your Google Business Profile that allows customers to ask questions about your business. Embracing this feature can help you provide helpful information and engage with potential customers effectively. Here's how to make the most of Google Q&A:

1. **Monitor Questions:** Regularly check your Q&A section for new questions from potential customers. Google often sends notifications, but it's a good practice to proactively monitor this section.

2. **Respond Promptly:** Provide prompt and accurate answers to questions. Quick responses demonstrate your commitment to customer service and can influence potential customers positively.

3. **Encourage Customers to Ask:** Encourage satisfied customers to ask questions in the Q&A section. This can help build a knowledge base that benefits future customers.

4. **Use Keywords:** When responding to questions, incorporate relevant keywords that potential customers might use in their queries. This can help improve the visibility of your profile in Google searches.

5. **Be Informative:** Offer detailed and informative answers to address customers' concerns. This helps build trust and positions your business as a reliable source of information.

6. **Correct Inaccurate Information:** If you come across incorrect information in the Q&A section, politely correct it. Ensuring the accuracy of information is essential for potential customers.

7. **Promote Services:** Use the Q&A section to highlight your products or services when relevant to a customer's question. This can subtly promote your offerings.

8. **Set Up FAQs:** Consider creating a frequently asked questions (FAQs) section in your Google Business Profile. This can preemptively address common queries and provide convenience to potential customers.

9. **Flag Inappropriate Content:** If you encounter inappropriate questions or answers, flag them for removal to maintain the integrity of your Q&A section.

Google Q&A is a powerful tool to engage with your audience, provide valuable information, and demonstrate your commitment to customer satisfaction. By actively participating in this feature, you can influence potential customers' decisions and enhance your business's online presence.

TIP 6: UTILIZE GOOGLE BUSINESS PROFILE MESSAGING

Google Business Profile Messaging is a direct communication channel between you and potential customers. By using this feature effectively, you can engage with inquiries, address concerns, and potentially convert leads into customers. Here's how to make the most of it:

1. **Enable Messaging:** Start by enabling the Messaging feature in your Google Business Profile settings. This allows customers to send you direct messages with their inquiries.

2. **Set Response Time:** Google allows you to set a response time for messages. Be realistic about how quickly you can respond and aim to maintain a quick response time. This demonstrates your commitment to customer service.

3. **Create Automated Responses:** Consider setting up automated responses for frequently asked questions or to acknowledge customer inquiries outside of your business hours. This ensures that customers receive a timely acknowledgment.

4. **Be Professional:** Maintain a professional and courteous tone in your messages. Remember that these interactions can influence potential customers' perceptions of your business.

5. **Provide Helpful Information:** When customers inquire about your products, services, or business details, offer clear and informative responses. Ensure that you answer their questions thoroughly.

6. **Encourage Appointments and Sales:** Use Messaging as an opportunity to schedule appointments, offer quotes, or guide potential customers toward making a purchase. Provide clear instructions on how to proceed.

7. **Privacy and Security:** Be cautious about sharing sensitive information through Messaging. Keep personal and financial details private and encourage customers to visit your official website or contact you through secure channels for such inquiries.

8. **Consistent Branding:** Ensure that your messaging interactions reflect your brand's values and identity. Consistency in messaging can help strengthen your brand image.

9. **Monitor and Respond Regularly:** Make it a routine to monitor your messaging platform and respond to inquiries promptly. A neglected messaging channel can deter potential customers.

10. **Request Reviews:** If you have positive interactions with customers through Messaging, kindly ask them to leave reviews on your Google Business Profile to share their positive experiences.

Google Business Profile Messaging is a convenient way to connect with potential customers in real-time, answer their questions, and guide them toward taking action. By providing excellent customer service through this channel, you can enhance your business's reputation and increase conversions.

TIP 7: HARNESS THE POWER OF GOOGLE INSIGHTS

Google provides valuable insights and analytics through your Google Business Profile, offering you data-driven information about how customers interact with your business online. Leveraging these insights can help you make informed decisions and continually improve your online presence. Here's how to use Google Insights effectively:

1. **Access Your Insights:** Log in to your Google My Business account and navigate to the Insights section. Here, you'll find a wealth of data about how users interact with your profile.

2. **Understand User Behavior:** Review metrics such as "Views," "Searches," and "Actions" to understand how users discover and engage with your business. These insights can help you tailor your content and strategies.

3. **Analyze Customer Actions:** Pay attention to the "Customer Actions" section, which shows what actions users took after finding your profile, including website visits, direction requests,

and phone calls.

4. **Track Popular Times:** Determine when your business is most popular among customers. This information can help you optimize your operating hours and staffing to accommodate peak times.

5. **Compare Periods:** Use the data to compare performance over different time periods. This can help you identify trends and assess the impact of changes you've made.

6. **Analyze Queries:** Discover the search terms that led users to your profile. This can provide insights into what customers are looking for and guide your keyword strategy.

7. **Review Photo Engagement:** Understand which photos are getting the most views and engagement. Use this information to curate a collection of appealing images that represent your business effectively.

8. **Monitor Audience Demographics:** Learn about the age groups, gender, and locations of your audience. Tailor your content and promotions to better resonate with your target demographics.

9. **Set Goals and KPIs:** Use the insights to set specific goals and key performance indicators (KPIs) for your Google Business Profile. Regularly review your progress toward these goals.

10. **Adjust Your Strategy:** Based on your findings, make data-driven adjustments to your profile, posts, and marketing strategies. Continually refine your approach to better meet the needs of your audience.

Google Insights is a powerful tool for understanding how your audience interacts with your Google Business Profile. By regularly reviewing and acting on this data, you can fine-tune your online presence, attract more customers, and ultimately grow your business. Stay tuned for more strategies to optimize your Google Business Profile!

TIP 8: OPTIMIZE FOR LOCAL SEO

Local search engine optimization (SEO) is crucial for businesses looking to attract customers in their local area. Optimizing your Google Business Profile for local SEO can help you rank higher in local search results and increase your visibility to potential customers. Here's how to do it:

1. **Accurate Business Information:** Ensure that all your business information, including name, address, phone number (NAP), and website URL, is accurate and consistent across all online platforms, including your Google Business Profile.

2. **Select Relevant Categories:** Choose the most relevant and specific categories for your business on your profile. Be as precise as possible to help Google understand your business.

3. **Write a Detailed Business Description:** Craft a comprehensive business description that includes relevant keywords and highlights your products, services, and unique selling points. Be concise and informative.

4. **High-Quality Photos:** Upload high-resolution photos that showcase your business, products, and services. Use descriptive filenames and alt text to make them more discoverable in searches.

5. **Collect Reviews:** Encourage satisfied customers to leave reviews on your Google Business Profile. Positive reviews can boost your local SEO rankings and build trust with potential customers.

6. **Use Keywords Strategically:** Incorporate relevant keywords into your profile's description, posts, and Q&A responses. Think about the terms customers might use to find businesses like yours in your local area.

7. **Geo-Tag Photos:** If applicable, geo-tag your photos with location information. This can help improve your profile's local relevance.

8. **Create Local Posts:** Use Google Posts to promote local events, specials, or promotions. Mention specific neighborhoods, landmarks, or local events in your posts to connect with your community.

9. **Add Local Phone Numbers:** If you have multiple locations, use local phone numbers for each branch. This can help customers in specific areas find and contact you more easily.

10. **Monitor and Respond to Local Feedback:** Keep an eye on local reviews and feedback. Address any concerns or questions from local customers promptly and professionally.

11. **Build Local Citations:** Ensure your business information is listed accurately on other online directories and platforms. Consistent citations can boost your local SEO efforts.

12. **Utilize Google Maps:** Embed Google Maps on your website to make it easy for customers to find your physical location. Include a clear call to action for directions.

Optimizing your Google Business Profile for local SEO is essential for attracting nearby customers who are actively searching for products or services like yours. By following these strategies, you can improve your local visibility, increase website traffic, and ultimately drive more foot traffic to your business.

TIP 9: SHOWCASE YOUR PRODUCTS AND SERVICES

Your Google Business Profile is an ideal platform to showcase your products and services effectively. By providing detailed information and compelling visuals, you can capture the attention of potential customers and influence their purchasing decisions. Here's how to make the most of this opportunity:

1. **Create Product Listings:** If you offer specific products, create individual product listings on your Google Business Profile. Include product names, descriptions, prices, and high-quality images. This is particularly valuable for retail businesses.

2. **Highlight Key Services:** Describe your primary services in detail. Explain what sets your services apart from competitors and why potential customers should choose you.

3. **Use Product and Service Posts:** Regularly use Google Posts to promote featured products, services, or special offers. Posts appear prominently in your profile and can attract attention.

4. **Update Availability:** If your product availability changes or you introduce new services, update your profile promptly to reflect these changes. This helps prevent customer confusion.

5. **Include Customer Reviews:** Encourage customers to leave reviews specifically related to your products or services. Positive reviews can reinforce the quality of what you offer.

6. **Use High-Quality Visuals:** Upload clear and engaging images of your products and services. Show them in use, highlight unique features, and provide a sense of scale when applicable.

7. **Provide Pricing Information:** When appropriate, include pricing information to give potential customers a clear idea of what to expect. This can help prequalify leads.

8. **Link to Relevant Pages:** If you have dedicated product or service pages on your website, link to them from your Google Business Profile. This can drive traffic to your site for more in-depth information.

9. **Utilize Google Shopping:** If you're an e-commerce business, consider using Google Shopping ads to showcase your products directly in search results.

10. **Create Service Menus:** For service-oriented businesses

like restaurants or salons, create service menus with detailed descriptions, prices, and any special offers.

11. **Highlight Special Features:** If your products or services have unique features, benefits, or certifications, make sure to mention them in your descriptions.

12. **Educate and Inform:** Use your profile to educate potential customers about how your products or services can meet their needs and solve their problems.

By effectively showcasing your products and services on your Google Business Profile, you can capture the interest of potential customers and guide them towards making informed decisions. This can lead to increased inquiries, bookings, and sales for your business. Stay tuned for more strategies to optimize your Google Business Profile!

TIP 10: FOSTER COMMUNITY ENGAGEMENT

Building a sense of community around your business can be a powerful way to connect with your audience, strengthen customer loyalty, and attract new customers. Here's how to foster community engagement through your Google Business Profile:

1. **Share Local Stories:** Highlight your involvement in the local community by sharing stories, events, or partnerships that demonstrate your commitment to the area where your business operates.

2. **Support Local Causes:** Show your support for local charities, causes, or events through your Google Business Profile. Mention your participation in community activities and encourage customers to get involved.

3. **Community Posts:** Use Google Posts to share news about local events, sponsorships, or initiatives that your business is a part of. These posts can generate interest and engagement from community members.

4. **Customer Spotlights:** Celebrate your loyal customers by featuring them on your profile. Share their success stories or experiences with your products or services.

5. **Respond to Local Reviews:** Engage with local customers by responding to their reviews, mentioning the specific neighborhood or location where they visited your business. This personal touch can strengthen local ties.

6. **Host Local Events:** If feasible, host or sponsor events in your community and promote them through your Google Business Profile. This can attract local attendees and create a sense of belonging.

7. **Use Local Lingo:** Use regional or local terminology in your posts and descriptions to resonate with the local audience. This shows that you understand and connect with the community.

8. **Highlight Local Partnerships:** If you collaborate with other local businesses or organizations, promote these partnerships on your profile. This can expand your reach within the community.

9. **Encourage User-Generated Content:** Encourage customers to share their experiences with your business by tagging you in their posts or using a specific hashtag. Feature user-generated content on your profile.

10. **Host Community Challenges:** Create fun and engaging challenges or contests related to your business and the local community. Encourage participation and offer prizes to winners.

11. **Provide Local Recommendations:** Offer local tips and recommendations, such as the best places to eat, visit, or shop in your area. This positions you as a valuable resource for local information.

12. **Engage in Local Conversations:** Respond to comments and engage in discussions related to your local community on your Google Business Profile. Show your active involvement in local matters.

Fostering community engagement through your Google Business Profile not only deepens your connection with local customers but also enhances your business's reputation and presence in the area. A strong sense of community can lead to customer loyalty, word-of-mouth referrals, and increased support from your local audience.

In conclusion, harnessing the power of your Google Business Profile can be a game-changer for your business. By following the tips and strategies outlined in this book, you're well on your way to maximizing your online presence, attracting new customers, and fostering strong relationships within your community.

Remember that your Google Business Profile is not static; it's a dynamic tool that can evolve with your business. Continually monitor, update, and refine your profile to stay ahead in the competitive digital landscape.

If you've found value in the insights shared in this book and would like further assistance in optimizing your Google Business Profile or managing your online presence, we're here to help. Visit our website at www.socialfunnelmarketing.com to explore our services and discover how our team of experts can assist you in achieving your business goals.

Whether you're looking to enhance your online visibility, engage with your audience, or simply take the hassle out of managing your Google Business Profile, our dedicated professionals are ready to support you every step of the way.

Thank you for taking the time to learn and grow with us. Here's to your business's continued success in the digital age!